A loser says "if only",
a winner says "next time".

It is a funny thing about life;
if you refuse to accept anything but the best,
you very often get it.

Small opportunities are often the beginning
of great enterprises.

A winner makes commitments;
a loser makes promises.

All things are difficult
before they are easy.

High risk, high reward!

Happiness lies in the job of achievement
and the thrill of creative effort.

F orget the past,
remember the future.

When you hire people who are smarter than you are, you prove you are smarter than they are.

Our chief want in life is somebody who will make us do what we can.

People forget how fast you did a job —
buy they remember how well you did it.

The man who wins
may have lost the wind several times,
but he never lets down his sails.

We are continually faced by great opportunities brilliantly disguised as insoluble problems.

A winner works hard
to achieve success,
a loser works hard
to find a shortcut to success.

Fast pay makes fast friends.

There's a special force
that gets people working as a team.
Once that force is in action
the team is virtually unbeatable.

The highest reward for a person's toil
is not what they get for it,
but what they become by it.

As I grow older, I pay less attention
to what men say.
I just watch what they do.

A winner goes through a problem;
a loser goes around it
and never gets beyond it.

To love what you do and feel that it matters...
how could anything be more fun?

The best skipper is the one
who has sense enough
to pick good men to do what he wants done,
and self-restraint enough
to keep from meddling with them while they do it.

Genius is one percent inspiration
and ninety-nine percent perspiration.

The price of greatness is responsibility.

No cash, no splash!

CARPENTER'S
BOAT REPAIR

27

Things may come to those who wait,
but only the things left by those who hustle.

The speed of the leader
determines the rate of the pack.

The difference between ordinary and extraordinary is that little extra.

Winners expect to win in advance.
Life is a self-fulfilling prophecy.

The reward of a thing well done
is to have done it.

A winner listens;
a loser just waits until it's his turn to talk.

The difference between a successful person
and others is not a lack of strength,
not a lack of knowledge,
but rather a lack of will.

Man's mind, once stretched by a new idea,
never regains its original dimensions.

It's hard to pass
while you follow in your competitor's footsteps.

When we have done our best,
we should wait the result in peace.

A winner says there ought to be a better way;
a loser says
that's the way it has always been.

A great pleasure in life
is doing what people say you cannot do.

No problem can stand the assault
of sustained thinking.

Failures are divided into two classes —
those who thought and never did
and those who did and never thought.

A ccept the challenges,
so that you may feel the exhilaration of victory.

When two men in a business always agree,
one of them is unnecessary.

Be careful what you ask for
because you might get it.

The man who believes he can do something
is probably right,
and so is the man who believes he can't.

There is something that is much more scarce,
something rarer than ability.
It is the ability to recognize ability.

Well done is better than well said.

A winner paces himself;
a loser has only two speeds:
hysterical and lethargic.

You snooze, you lose.

Attitude, performance, teamwork and competition...
these are the raw materials
that go into the act of winning.

Many receive advice,
only the wise profit from it.

The future belongs to those who believe in their dreams.

Progress always involves risk;
while you strategically navigate,
you also have to sail with your instincts.

The better you know your strengths
and capitalize on them,
the better you'll do competitively.

Genius is the ability
to reduce the complicated to the simple.

Winning is an excellent measure of success.

Success is a journey,
not a destination.

Success is simply a matter of luck.
Ask any failure.

Do not wish to be anything
but what you are,
and try to be that perfectly.

It's hard to hear the music
when you blow your own horn.

Obstacles are those frightful things you see
when you take your eyes off your goals.

A winner says "let's find out";
a loser says "nobody knows".

Luck is what happens
when preparation meets opportunity.

One man with courage
makes a majority.

The quality of a person's life
is in direct proportion to their commitment
to excellence,
regardless of their chosen field of endeavor.

May the most you desire
be the least you receive.

D_{on't} wait for your ship to come in,
swim out to it!

The secret of happiness is not in doing what one likes, but in liking what one does.

A winner works harder than a loser
and has more time;
a loser is always too busy
to do what is necessary.

A winner isn't nearly as afraid of losing as a loser is secretly afraid of winning.

Destiny is not a matter of chance,
it is a matter of choice.

Excellence implies more than competence...
it implies a striving for the highest possible standards.

JOIN DENNIS CONNER'S WINNING TEAM

Dear Dennis:

I am interested in learning more about the America's Cup and Dennis Conner Sports' many sailing related products and activities. Please put me on your mailing list so that I can stay informed.

I am especially interested in:

☐ America's Cup
☐ Whitbread Round the World Race
☐ USA Yacht Club

☐ DC Merchandise
☐ Other DC books
☐ Other

Name: _____

Address: _____

City, State & Zip: _____

Mr. Dennis Conner
DENNIS CONNER SPORTS, INC.
720 Gateway Center Drive, Suite E
San Diego, CA 92102

Other Titles by Great Quotations Publishing Company
COMB BOUND

A Friend Is
A Smile Increases Your Face Value
Aged to Perfection
An Apple A Day
Backfield in Motion
Batter Up
Bedside Manner
Believe and Achieve
Best in Business Humor
Birthday Wishes
Books Are Better
Boyfriends Live Longer Than Husbands
Change Your Thoughts,
   Change Your Life
Don't Marry, Be Happy
Double Dribble
Golf Humor
Graduation - Keys To Success
Great Quotes - Great Comedians
Halfway Home (Surviving
   the Middle Years)
Harvest Of THoughts
Inspirations
Joy Of Family
Keys To Happiness
Life's Winning Tips
Love, Honor, Cherish
Love, Sex & Marriage
Love On Your Wedding Day
Mothers And Babies
Never Give Up
Our Life Together

Over The Hill Sex
Political Humor
Quotations from African-American
Real Friends
Retirement
Sports Poop
Sports Quotes
Stress
Teachers Inspirations
Thank You
The Quest For Success
Things You'll Learn
Thinking Of You
Thoughts From The Heart
To A Very Special Daughter
To A Very Special Son
To A Very Special Grandparent
To A Very Special Love
To My Mother
To My Father
Unofficial Christmas Survival Guide
Unofficial Executive Survival Guide
Unofficial Stress Test
Unofficial Survival Guide
   · to Parenthood
Unofficial Vacation Guide
Ordinary Men, Extraordinary Lives
Our Thoughts Are Prayers
What To Tell Your Children
Who Really Said
Wonders & Joys Of Christmas
Words From Great Women

PAPERBACK

199 Useful Things to Do With
  A Politician
201 Best Things Ever Said
A Lifetime of Love
A Light Heart Lives Long
A Teacher Is Better Than Two Books
As A Cat Thinketh
Cheatnotes On Life
Chicken Soup
Dear Mr. President
Father Knows Best
Food For Thought
Golden Years/Golden Words
Happiness Walks On Busy Feet
Heal The World
Hooked on Golf
Hollywords
I'm Not Over The Hill

In Celebration of Women
Life's Simple Pleasures
Mother - A Bouquet of Love
Motivation Magic
Mrs. Webster's Dictionary
Reflections
Romantic Rendezvous
Sports Page
So Many Ways To Say
  Thank You
The ABC's of Parenting
The Best Of Friends
The Birthday Astrologer
The Little Book of
  Spiritual Wisdom
Things You'll Learn,
  If You Live Long Enough

PERPETUAL CALENDARS

Apple A Day
Country Proverbs
Each Day A New Beginning
Friends Forever
Golf Forever
Home Is Where The Heart Is
Proverbs
Seasonings
Simply The Best Dad
Simple The Best Mom
Simple Ways To Say I Love You

Teacher"s" Are "First Class!"

Great Quotations Publishing Company
1967 Quincy Court
Glendale Heights, IL 60139-2045
Phone (708) 582-2800
FAX (708) 582-2813